Finding Me

AF624694

Mirette Abraham

BookLeaf Publishing

Finding Me © 2022 Mirette Abraham

All rights reserved.

No part of this publication may be reproduced, stored in a retrieval system, or transmitted, in any form or by any means, electronic, mechanical, photocopying, recording or otherwise, without the prior written permission of the presenters.

Mirette Abraham asserts the moral right to be identified as author of this work.

Presentation by *BookLeaf Publishing*

Web: www.bookleafpub.com

E-mail: info@bookleafpub.com

ISBN: 978-93-95784-94-8

First edition 2022

Dedicated to you.

You who are searching.

You who are found.

You who are hopeful.

You who are fearful.

You in your highs,

and you in your lows.

All of you.

Why Here?

I've sat and pondered on my life's purpose,
I still think about that a lot,
I wonder why I've been put on this earth,
Why in this very particular spot?

I've dedicated years to seeking this out
And lost nights of unrest,
All to try and uncover the reason
I've been given this specific test.

Am I doing this right? Am I in the right lane?
Am I heading in the right direction?
Do I make a turn here or do I just stay the
course?
My mind races with so many questions.

People will tell you, "trust in God,
And He will show you the way,"
But I still worry about the steps in between
The ones He's given me free will to take.

I wonder if I take a wrong step
Will I alter the course of my life's path
And if I mess up along the way
Is there any way to find a way back?

But in the end, you know it doesn't matter
Which way you turn or go
For whatever you choose, even by mistake
God's glory can still overflow.

So, don't seek out those answers
Just entrust Him with every step
And soon enough you'll see for yourself
That you got to the place, only with His help.

Existence

The days were short
the memories distant
and change resisted.
But now the days are long
the memories lived together
and we no longer remember the 'we' that
existed.

Instead, we live through them,
for them mostly,
as though they rely on our breath to live.
But daily they remind us
that they too are making memories
some apart from you and me.

We try to live
outside this box we made home
to find ourselves again.
But honestly, my love,
no matter where we go
it is you I find my purpose in.

So, although the days were short
and the memories distant
and dramatic change we resisted,

now in the longer days
and the living of memories together
I'm finding that you're the reason for my
existence.

In the Waiting

Lord, I am growing weary in my waiting.
Waiting on Your plan.
Waiting on Your hand.
Waiting on You.

I look for solace in empty wells,
Desperate for reassurance
That someone is coming to find me.

The alleyways are dark and lonesome,
Filled with the cries of those
Who once walked these same roads.
Nothing but questions plaster their walls,
And the pavement etched
With thousands of footprints.
We've all somehow made it here
And ironically gone nowhere else
Despite never having stopped walking.

I've come to the place of no rest,
Of no peace or comfort.
Simply because I ran away from my waiting
Afraid of the pain it might bring forth.

I waited for what seemed like a lifetime
Growing weary and spent.
But if I had hung on to that rope a little longer,
The Lord I may have met.

It seems that my running away
Has halted my journey
And brought an end to my struggles and joys alike.

So, Lord, guide me back to my waiting
I'm ready to commit
For in the weariness I'll find
Beauty in the grit.

Why Didn't You Tell Me?

People warned me about a lot
Of the changes that I'll see
They warned me of all the storms
But they failed to mention the change in me

They told me of the sleepless nights
And of the added financial stress
They told me of the baby's habits
And even of the avalanching mess

They told me about my relationships
And how they won't be the same
How the people I learn to trust now
Will be different to the ones who before them
came

They told me too of all the pain
And how it just lingers without cause
They warned me of the guilt that doesn't fade
And how I will only be seeing my flaws

But they failed to mention all the changes
In the person of myself, I once knew before
That came with this new life-changing role

The day I became known as 'Mum' and nothing more

I've failed harder than I've ever imagined
But continue to fight for those left in my care
I've sunk to emotional depths I've only ever heard of
But carried on with my day as though the struggle wasn't there

I've held on so tightly to people I could have only dreamt of
But I've given myself permission to let them bleed
I've been cut so deep by wounds only I could see
But I've covered it up so others don't see me in need

I'm not the me I used to be
I'm being refined and I'm being made new
I can't wait to see how God uses this broken vessel for more
And to get to know the one who now wears my shoes

It Was Always You

It was never me Lord, but You.

You turn my sins into grace.
You turn my grief into joy.
You turn my brokenness into a vessel of light.
You turn my nothingness into glory.
You turn me toward You.

See Your Through Them

To be able to see yourself through their eyes,
Would make all the difference!

They see past the flaws.
They see past the imperfections.
They see past the moments of weakness.
They see past the bravery and embrace you in your falls.

They only see the love, the sacrifice and Christ Himself
In everything and everyone.
And they unconditionally pour their whole selves onto us every day.

Oh, to one day notice the God who does just that and more!

He sees beauty in the flaws.
He sees eternal value in the imperfections.
He sees such strength in those moments of weakness.
He gives only His grace in the pits we too often fall into.

He sees love.
He sees me.

Stillness in the Storm

I looked outside
But all I could see,
Was the pile of chores
Waiting for me.

I peeped into your room
Wanting to watch you play,
But all I could appreciate
Is the added work to my day.

I snuck into the kitchen
To whip you up a meal,
But I choked on my overwhelm
And the joy that it did steal.

I took a seat on the lounge
Trying to regain my calm,
But all I managed to notice
Was the pile of laundry beneath my arm.

The day passed on by
As swiftly as a brief storm,
And the only thing I remember
Is how badly I felt worn.

I don’t recall the sunshine
And I can’t remember your dress.
I can only bring to mind the chaos,
And the unforgiving mess.

You asked me if I’m ok
And honestly sweetie, I’m not sure,
But seeing the warmth in your smile,
I don’t really mind anymore.

I pray I can learn to look past it all
And take you in while I can.
I pray our Lord can still this storm inside
And use me in His greater plan.

I pray for gratitude
I pray for peace
I pray for stillness in this storm
I pray, O Lord, please.

Put On Love

How much nicer would life be,
If we all stood by each other;
If we all lived for one another;
If we all loved each other with the love and light of Christ?

Here's to you, mama,
For loving beyond your capacity.

Here's to you, mama,
For giving more than you have.

Here's to you, mama,
For laying aside your pride for your loves.

Here's to you, mama,
For embracing others and making them feel included.

Here's to you, mama,
For checking in when you really have no strength.

Here's to you, mama,
For pouring your heart when you're running on empty.

Here's to you, mama,
For putting aside your judgements and choosing to learn.

Here's to you, mama,
For holding on to your dreams, but not worrying about timing.

Here's to you, mama,
For constantly throwing away your comfort in the name of love.

Here's to you, mama,
For putting off your old self to allow our God to transform you.

Here's to you, mama,
For being the embodiment of that very word – Mama.

Today, I choose to offer myself up.
I choose to fill another's cup.
I choose to keep my eyes focused above.

And above all,
I choose to put on love.

Colossians 3:12-15:
Therefore, as the elect of God, holy and beloved, put on tender mercies, kindness, humility, meekness, longsuffering; bearing with one another, and forgiving one another, if anyone has a complaint against another; even as Christ forgave you, so you also must do. But above all these things put on love, which is the bond of perfection. And let the peace of God rule in your hearts, to which also you were called in one body; and be thankful.

Moment

What's your moment?

Have you realized your moment yet?
Amidst the chaos and the mundanity of every
day, have you noticed Him moulding you?
You ask what the point of all of this is, and the
answer, friend, is to prepare you for your
moment.
There's a moment when you finally see why
you're here.
There's a moment when you can truly appreciate
where the Lord wants you to be.
There's a moment when you start to see your
worth, and better even, your worth through the
eyes of your Maker.

So, maybe for you,
this moment right now,
where you feel overwhelmed and underprepared,
is the exact moment that'll bring glory to His
name.

Rest

Today I rest easy.

Not because of anything I've done.
Or anything I'm yet to do.
But because of you.

My body fails me daily.
And my mind runs short little sprints that never seem to get me to that finish line.
I'm constantly burdened by fear.
By pain.
By noise.

And yet, here you stand.
With nothing but pure joy in front of me.
Happy to see me at the end of your tiresome day.
Your embrace is filled with comfort.
With peace.
With rest.

I'll never know why I was chosen for you.
God knows I fall short every day.
Your mere presence is enough to drive away the day's troubles.

It’s failures.
It’s sadness.

The day comes to a close with you wrapped in my arms.
You hold me close as your eyes surrender to sleep.
In your warmth I find my place.
My heart.
My reason.

So, I will rest easy.

Not because of anything I’ve done.
Or anything I’m yet to do.
But because of you.

In Her Middle

She remained in the middle.

Her middle moments
waited for both the leaves to grow
and the frosty winter snow.

They longed for joy
but all the waiting
forced time into the fading.

She remained in the middle,
always longing,
never living.

Waiting

In the waiting, she found rest.
Not the physical kind.
No.
A much greater kind.

In the waiting, she found comfort.
Not the tangible kind.
No.
A much subtler kind.

In the waiting, she found strength.
Not enough to help her up.
No.
But enough to keep going.

In the waiting, she found peace.
Not from answered prayers.
No.
But in their absence.

In the waiting, she found Him.
The One whose glory was revealed
in her waiting.

You're All I See

My eyelids are heavy
My back aches
My tummy is rumbling
Mama, are you awake?

I hear you fumble
Rushing to get to me
I feel your constant wondering
If there is more that you could be.

But, mama, I wish you knew
Your place in my heart
You are my whole world
My everything, from life's start.

Your face smells of flowers,
Your chest breathes warmth,
Your kisses heal everything,
Your embrace calms storms.

I rest in your arms
And feel your love envelop me,
I gaze into your weary eyes,
Mama, you're all I see.

Your eyelids are heavy
And your back aches
Your tummy is rumbling
But you press on for my sake.

Holy Work

In the middle of the night,
When you're the only thing in sight,
My ears adjust to your frequency,
As I convince my body to not fail me.

Weary-eyed and heavy-heeled,
I make my way to meet your needs.
The darkness serves my tunnel vision,
For I only have one mission.

The daytime hours feel the same,
Keeping you happy is the only aim,
Cooking, cleaning, playing and repeat,
Never really having a seat.

The days, the weeks, and months go by,
And some moments I can't help but cry,
I love my life so much and don't want to
complain,
But so much mundanity can be hard to sustain.

I want to see purpose in my day,
I want to bring God glory in some way,
But sometimes it's hard to see
How dishes can satisfy that need.

In my sorrow, while I do another load
I hear the Lord call me as I fold,
"There is beauty in your mundanity child"
"But how is that true?" I replied

He said, "Whether it's a dish you clean,
And heart you make feel seen,
It's truly holy work, you see,
For your motherhood is glorifying Me."

Big Feelings

I wonder what life would be like,
If adults shared big feelings about life.
Would we all throw our bodies on the floor,
Or stomp our feet and slam those doors?

My toddler couldn't contain herself tonight,
Expressing sadness and anger while I held her tight.
She really had no particular reason,
Nor was this a difficult season.

But she just got wrapped up in her exhaustion,
Realising that she had bottled in so much emotion.
Throughout her long and tiring day,
There was nobody around to tell her she was ok.

She longed for a long hug,
And a whole lot of love.
She wished to be held for a little while,
And for a warm and comforting smile.

How many of us wish to be held
On those days when we feel completely spent?

Or when we’ve been beaten down at work all day,
To have someone just love us and say,

“You are loved and so very dear.
You are all I need right here.
You are enough even when you feel low.
You are the strongest, you need to know.”

The God Who Sees

You see our fears.
You see our strengths.
You see our pain.
You see our joy.
You see our anxiety.
You see our hope.
You see our shortcomings.
You see our talents.

You see us.
All of us.
And You love us all the same.

Distracted

I look out into the living room, but all I can see
is the mess.

Your toys scattered like confetti on the carpet.
Dishes that held everything you didn't want to
try creating a pile high enough to compete with
your lego tower.
Your books laid out on the floor instead of their
designated shelf, maybe wanting to use them as
stepping blocks in your 'floor is lava' game.
Clothes and shoes dressing the living room
furniture instead of the matching hangers I had
tirelessly picked out for your room.

Everything blurs my vision and distracts me
from you.

You ask me to play with you, but I need this
mess sorted first.
You ask me to read you a book, but I need this
managed so I can see the words clearly.
You ask me to help you play dress-ups, but I
can't fathom the thought of more clothes making
their way out here.

You ask me for my attention, but sadly it is very far from you right now.

What is it about the mess that distracts us from our children?
Why is it that housework makes us believe that our children are the ones in our way while we try and manage it?

Your toys, my love, bring you joy.
Those dishes, my love, have filled your belly.
The books, my love, have fuelled your imagination.
All the clothes, my love, have clothed your thriving body.

My love, you are more important.
And although sometimes it seems as though I've forgotten, know that I am trying and will continue to learn from you in this journey we now share.

I Know You

I know you in your tender touch,
And I see your gentleness within.
I know you in your stubbornness,
And I see the zeal you bring.

I know you in your sweet, soft kiss,
And I see your love shine bright.
I know you in your jumbled emotions,
And I see you'll set the world alight.

I know you in your warm embrace,
And I see the passion in your soul.
I know you in your tears of fear,
And I see its weight take its toll.

I know you in your infectious smile,
And I see the kindness inside.
I know you in your screams of anger,
And I see your fierceness take a stride.

I know you in every state,
And I see the person you'll be.
One that serves and loves with everything,
And takes the world by storm, you'll see!

So, hold firm to our Lord above,
He'll show you how to walk His way.
Be present in the moments He brings,
And in His love forever stay.

Rest assured I will never leave,
But one day I'll need to let go.
Don't worry you'll never be alone,
You'll just need space to learn and grow.

I will be right here until you're ready,
To take on the world even though it seems
tougher.
Because my love, I know you,
And I see how much you have to offer.

Seeing Him in the Pain

I often wonder "why?"

Why did I receive this trial?
Why did I receive this child?
Why did I feel so alone?
Why did I not feel the Lord come?

Why would He let me suffer?
Why, what more could I have offered?
Why do I feel the same sadness each day?
Why won't the hurt just go away?

Why would God not grant me this request?
Why, is this prayer not for the best?
Why can't I shake the despair?
Why is He not here when I'm so scared?

But I found the constant in all of these cries,
And that is the self-focus and the lies.
My Lord never left me, no, not at all,
But I was too preoccupied to notice His love
sprawled.

When all I can see is my pain,
My vision becomes strained.

And I become less able to see Him standing there,
With arms wide open, and His warmth of care.

You see, He never leaves, but instead, inches nearer,
To give me opportunities to see Him clearer.
But if I never cast my gaze off my fears,
My Lord will forever seem not near.

Asking Differently

I prayed for a miracle today.
But it never came.

In honesty, I prayed for the same one daily
And with each passing day, my hope was being
drowned by my reality.
But I got up and prayed anyway.
Only this time, I prayed differently.

Part of me wanted to hear God scream the
answer at me,
And all of me wanted that answer to be "Yes!"

Yes, to ending my pain.
Yes, to having my heart mended.
Yes, to making me happy.
Yes, to claiming my life back.

But today, I just knelt before Him.

Instead of asking Him to remove my pain,
I asked Him to make it mould me.
Instead of asking Him to mend my heart,
I asked Him to make it yearn for Him.
Instead of asking Him to make me happy,

I asked Him to let me see and feel His joy all around me.
Instead of asking Him to make things normal again,
I asked Him to touch everything and make it all extraordinary.

I didn't pray for the same miracle,
But I did get a more desirable gift.

I was freed of the mindset that what I want, and needed, is the right thing for me.
The weight of my expectations began to slowly and timidly trickle off my shoulders,
And what replaced it was the sureness of my Saviour's love.

He knows me.
He loves me.
I just needed to ask differently.

"You ask and do not receive, because you ask amiss, that you may spend it on your pleasures."
– James 4:3

Dear Husband

Do you remember?

Do you remember when all our worries revolved around us;
Where we would live, work or eat?
Or when we would fall asleep on the couch watching a boring movie,
Too tired and lazy to leave our seats.

Do you remember having more time to read,
Write and sleep?
Or when our belongings, our money and our minds
Were all ours to keep.

Do you remember travelling the world,
And seeing sights we had only seen in our imaginations?
Or spontaneously booking trips and getaways
And having the freedom to go on any vacation.

But do you remember the unspoken emptiness
That we never actually took notice of?
Or the longing and yearning
To share our abundance of love.

Do you remember the stillness and the prayers
And desires it so desperately wished for.
Or the quiet that filled our home and hearts,
Even though we both wanted to say more.

Do you remember thinking that our hearts
Could have exploded when we first saw her?
Or the change in the character of both
Our pains and laughter.

Do you remember the unexpected sweetness that came
with the dramatic change in our life?
Or the beauty that broke through
The seams of our strife.

Could you have ever imagined
Love and beauty so profound?
Or how differently our hearts skip
Every time she makes a sound.

Can you even picture a life,
Like the one we had before?
One void of all this beautiful chaos
And love that keeps trickling in more.

I can't wait for all that's waiting
To come our way;
All the laughter and pain,
And everything our life still wants to say.

All the love, the hurt,
The joyous moments and the painful ones too;
I can't wait to do them all
With you.

www.ingramcontent.com/pod-product-compliance
Lightning Source LLC
Chambersburg PA
CBHW051746130826
49812CB00033B/1022
9789395784948